MARTIN LUTHER KING, JR.
CHANGING LIVES

WRITTEN BY PATRICE GOTSCH

ILLUSTRATED BY GIL ARREOLA

To Ted Gotsch and Phyllis Young, who taught me so much
about the inspiration of Dr. Martin Luther King, Jr.
Patrice Gotsch

For Liz, Cari, and Tiff, three strong young women whose ability
to overcome life's obstacles and whose strength to move forward
inspire me to dream of and work toward a better world.
Gil Arreola

Editor
Dr. Roberta Stathis

Art Direction and Design
Danielle Arreola

Editorial Staff
Kristin Belsher
Linda Mammano
Rebecca Ratnam
Nina Chun

Printing Coordinator
Cathy Sanchez

Ballard & Tighe

The life of Dr. Martin Luther King, Jr. illustrates how one man's dream can change a nation.

I Have A Dream

"... I have a dream that one day this nation will rise up and live out the true meaning of its **creed:** *'We hold these truths to be self-evident: that all men are created equal.'"*

These words rang loud and clear on August 28, 1963, when King delivered one of the most famous speeches in American history. King's journey to become the greatest American civil rights leader was not an easy one.

creed: a statement of belief

A Religious Upbringing

Martin Luther King, Jr. was born January 15, 1929, in Atlanta, Georgia. Martin's father was a Baptist preacher. The church was a major part of the King family's life.

Facing Racism

Throughout his childhood, Martin faced **racism** against black Americans. He learned early on that black Americans did not have the same rights as white Americans. This made young Martin angry. However, his parents always reminded him that "it was my duty as a Christian to love ...," even to love people who did not love him.

racism: feelings or actions of hatred toward a person or persons because of their race

A Love of Learning

Before he could even read, young Martin surrounded himself with books. He also was fascinated by language and sounds and the way they could be used to **inspire** people. Martin skipped two grades and entered Morehouse College when he was 15 years old.

inspire: to encourage

Dr. and Mrs. Martin Luther King, Jr.

Martin graduated from college in 1948. Then he decided to study religion at Crozer Theological Seminary. He attended graduate school at Boston University and earned a doctorate in theology in 1955. While in Boston, he married Corretta Scott.

Change Is Possible!

King became the pastor of Dexter Avenue Baptist Church in Montgomery, Alabama. King's religious beliefs and education convinced him that change was possible, and he began his journey to end racism and fight for equal rights for all Americans. Most importantly, King believed that these goals could be achieved through nonviolent actions.

Segregation in America

King believed that segregation was a major problem in society. He said, "Men often hate each other because they fear each other; they fear each other because they do not know each other; they do not know each other because they cannot communicate; they cannot communicate because they are separated."

Rosa Parks and the Bus Boycott

On December 1, 1955, the police arrested a woman named Rosa Parks. What crime did she commit? She was tired after a long day at work. She refused to give up her seat on a Montgomery city bus to a white person. Black civil rights leaders, led by King, decided to organize a **boycott** of the buses. The boycott lasted for more than a year.

boycott: the act of refusing
to buy, use, or sell something

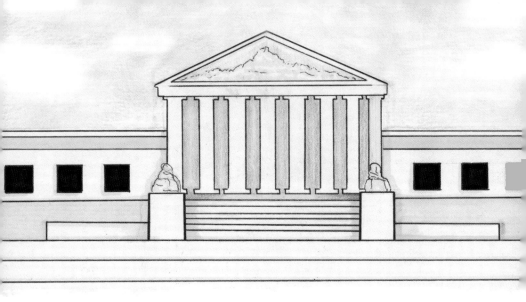

A Major Step to End Segregation

The boycott finally ended when the United States Supreme Court ordered the city of Montgomery to provide **integrated** seating on public buses. This was a major step in the fight to end segregation, but it came with a price. During the boycott, King's home was bombed, he was arrested, and he experienced much **abuse**.

abuse: mistreatment; injury
integrated: free and equal association; not segregated or separate

A Civil Rights Leader

King was a powerful and inspirational public speaker. Both blacks and whites who believed in his cause joined the civil rights movement. He was elected president of the Southern Christian Leadership Conference, an organization formed to support the civil rights movement.

Organizing Nonviolent Demonstrations

As a civil rights leader, King organized many nonviolent demonstrations in the American South. People saw pictures of and read about King's demonstrations, and more and more people began to support his work.

demonstration: a public show of opinion

"I Have A Dream"

In August 1963, King led a march of more than 200,000 people in Washington, D.C. He delivered his speech at the Lincoln Memorial. In this speech, he said: "I have a dream that my four little children will one day live in a nation where they will not be judged by the color of their skin but by the content of their character."

The Civil Rights Act of 1964

King's efforts helped convince Congress to pass the Civil Rights Act of 1964. This law made it illegal for businesses to **discriminate** against people because of race, color, religion, or national origin. This law also gave the attorney general the power to end segregation in schools. King's dream was beginning to come true.

discriminate: to treat differently

The Work Continues

King's life was cut short on April 4, 1968, when he was shot and killed in Memphis, Tennessee. While King's life has ended, his dream lives on and the work he began continues. Dr. Martin Luther King, Jr. is an inspiration to all who believe that change is necessary and possible. In 1983, his birthday was made a national holiday.

HIS DREAM LIVES ON

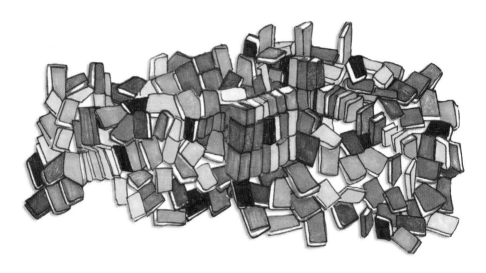